BLACK ACHILLES

# BLACK ACHILLES

Poems by
Curtis L. Crisler

Accents Publishing • Lexington, Kentucky • 2015

Copyright © 2015 by Curtis L. Crisler
All rights reserved

Printed in the United States of America

Accents Publishing
Editor: Katerina Stoykova-Klemer
Cover Image: *Study of legs,* Titian, 1557

ISBN: 978-1-936628-32-2
First Edition

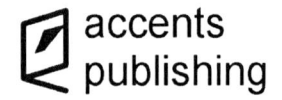

accents publishing

Accents Publishing is an independent press for brilliant voices. For a catalog of current and upcoming titles, please visit us on the Web at

www.accents-publishing.com

This is in reverence for the disabled, and their everyday life and fight.

## CONTENTS

★

Overseer  /  1
Black Achilles  /  2
You almost kill your mother and yourself  /  4
Carol for Another Christmas  /  5

★

Why play b-ball at forty-eight  /  9
There's this …  /  15
An inconvenient truth  /  16
Nag  /  17

★

Date night  /  21
Where the brain goes  /  22
hobbler ode  /  26

*Notes / Acknowledgments / About the Author  /  27*

"the wheelchairs hate the shoes"

## OVERSEER

Inconvenience puts his arms around me. This hug
weighs world-winds and begs like infidelity's lip-

stick marks. He wants me to learn how to fall again.
There's no sophistication to hitting the ground. I do

it harder now, not like sad demigods. Now, I aim
for couches, beds, and the carpet instead of linoleum

floors. I am pissant marvelous, distracting a biting
splint in my leg. I never knew walking my obstacle,

and all those in wheelchairs, with canes, with no
limbs make me feel the sacrilege against collagen,

the separating of myself; me against me, my taut
tendon breaking itself in two. Inconvenience puffs

out his chest, proud in making me flounder to the
ground. I heard Inconvenience put hands on Lucifer

to spark fires. He bends me over for reclamation,
to do it all again, to let me know what tender means.

## BLACK ACHILLES

This god has fallen
My damn fingers go against me
Work to keep me balanced on new appendages

Crutches guide me now
It is good if I don't misinterpret my new swagger
How I once feared nothing—heartache, gun shots, tsunamis

I now fear stairs
I have counted them out—13
Down and up, all the superstitions

I have left myself to gain more of myself
Finding myself in another mindset—a carnival game
And like all carnival games, the house was against me

I could not win, have learned the creaky banister a friendly
Like some adventurer it holds me up, as I hear my neighbors'
Voices behind closed doors

I don't want them to see me like this, flailing, obnoxious
I don't want their hands of assistance
I want my tendon healed

Zeus cannot see this, so turns his head
Elohim cannot see this, so smiles at me
Kali cannot see this, so empowerment's limp

The Coyote will not regurgitate the sun, or howl at me
I beseech them all, anything to get back to me
There is no compromise

I must do the work, so I transform into something strange
Something like Doc Octopus, with impediments
Ready to avenge all my shortcomings

## YOU ALMOST KILL YOUR MOTHER AND YOURSELF

on the first snow storm of the year. The state trooper releases you back into the elements with hardened words after you have done figure eights on I-69 south. The band saw nurses buzz their

blue beauty of care into your smile. *Why are you smiling?* The anesthesiologist blocks your left leg, gives your spine the needle that numbs your bottom half, all to repair the partially ruptured

tendon named after a demigod. You regurgitate a color wheel from cheese crackers and sprite, in the face of an unflinching mother and frenetic nurses. To siphon down your bladder from

the pressure to keep you hydrated, the catheter snaked into the urethra of your penis by the friendly nurses does not agitate you, for your bottom half was still comatose. You fill two containers

with the liquid from your insides. You just want to go home to release more piss. You barely get back into your own driveway. The snow punishes you like a Saturday bully looking for Sugar

Babies. You want your mother too. To come back down and get you from your SUV, while you watch ghosts escape your mouth. The air feels like ice cubes freezing. A neighbor assists in getting

you and your crutches through crunching snow. Left leg's still numb from the block. You elevate it against a halo of Christmas lights. *Where is the angel?* As you wait for your eyes to blacken.

## CAROL FOR ANOTHER CHRISTMAS

Surgery and inconvenience is a primordial
Cyclops. It's the all-in-ones flourishing
like gnats, all up in your face, as you swing
wildly at invisible opponents. The pinging
pain is from strong splint, where the fusing
of a tendon (an earthworm split in halves)
makes itself new from a doctor's apothecary
mysticism. Every time I wiggle my toes, I
forget I own them at all. The splint is so
strict, it numbs my leg, becomes restrictor.
My mother assists convalescence, like she
founded the Red Cross, 'til she rocks to sleep,
snoring notes I can see above her head. I am
back to a boy in tenement on gritty side of
life, suffering from pneumonia on Christmas
Eve. There are ointments for my chest, hot
toddies coat my throat, and a rancid vaccine
brawls with mean germs, viruses. This year,
this Christmas Eve, this now, Mama cannot
stand me up. I am sideswiped for a month,
two, maybe three. I will gain mobility back.
I will shoot from the top of the key, again.
Surgery and inconvenience will fade like cars
on the distant horizon where heat monkeys
play. Before the giant vanishes, I need to cut
him down, turn into Odysseus the Cunning,
overcorrect any vacillation on confidences.

*

## WHY PLAY B-BALL AT FORTY-EIGHT

*a)*

there's no women to conquer
    no boys to macho against
        no refs
            no contracts
                no scoreboard tall enough
                    to keep you away from swish

*b)*

there's no recruiters,
    no Lakers, 76ers, Cavaliers
        knocking the knocker on
            your mother's tattered door

there's that voice in your head
    the one that says "be a star"
        since the first dribble, it's been on

*c)*

there's no money
    no riding the bench
        no playing point
            no shooting forward
                no sixth man

the money you see, bills
    "pay for partially torn Achilles"
        pay for that pop
            that echo chamber in body
                that still-relevant ringing
                    that singeing in ears

*d)*

that singeing in ears
    is a silent monk tugging
        the bell tower's tongue,
            blabbing to the outliers,
                a voice for a light,
                    some reverence only
                        a woman naked without
                            frustration spills on you

*e)*

frustration spills on
    you like Jackson, Pop, Riley,
        making plays for a last minute
            Hack-a-Shack, like any child
                on any court when the sun
                    goes down….
                        "5…4…3…2…1"

*f)*
"5…4…3…2…1,"
    your mantra, your reason to
        juke, shake-n-bake, bring
            your "A" game since mama's
                calling your name, and this will
                    be the shot of the night as
                        the street lights blink…blink….

## THERE'S THIS ...

on each hand, brown sores gaining their scabs,
calling back puncture wounds where needles
needed entrance. Scarred. The spinal anesthesia

punching. *Is this like aftermath of acupuncture?*
The whore baths in the sink instead of showers.
The stress over surgical site infections. Scarred.

The bills for Ortho, for Emergency, for physicians,
for follow-ups. The knee carts. The cumbersome
crutches. The prayers for full mobility to return.

Scarred. There's the little stalls, the reaching for
the soap while on two new metal appendages.
How basic science can hold you up. As Doctor

Octavius, you have one flat tire—one appendage
disengaged—you can do nothing in your mania
to stop Spidey. Scarred. The stress of another fail.

The thinking, *Could I have done this without
the surgery?* The scared you own. Feeling your
Jesus-forsaken woe. There's this. There's this.

## AN INCONVENIENT TRUTH

There's this long magic about black & white
films that make me want to cuddle up inside

the grayness of the moments. There's rhythm
about the single yellow calling-light from the

window of the rural colonial house I pass by
on night rides on Interstates 30 & 69 back to

home. Why do I want to enter into the souls
of so many filaments & pixels I see in three

dimensions, letting my wanderer loose? Maybe
I am one single star in this galaxy, caught in

blackness, over a farmer's field of soybeans.
Maybe I'm a wandering urban legend wanting

the mundane of simplicity. There is no nostalgia
lingering in this. There is only the multiplicity

of moments, connections to connections to
connections. How I am connected to them all,

like Seurat's pointillism, like jazz, like sand. I'm
going on & on to the break of dawn, & some.

# NAG

Inconvenience is hungry and wonders where
we are going to eat today, this Wednesday night,

the third Wednesday since my Achilles popped like
a bullet leaving from a gun inside a car held in the

hands of a man caught in revenge's clutch. A drive-
by. My failed defense. A rupture with no rapture.

I had fallen down on myself—tumbled like clean
laundry stacked up high—then pushed to crumple.

The echo chamber of my body, a magnificent Bose
speaker, replicated a funnel of sound. Somehow

I could still hobble like monsters do. I limped back
to sideline starting the last start I would start for

a basketball squad. This is where inconvenience
introduced himself, like a Vietnam vet from streets,

a sergeant who talks to recruits no one sees but
him. I had been stuck with him for a week, and he

was a taker of energy, only eats souls dipped in an
au jus. What I couldn't stomach was this pulsing

in my tendon, the stolen time from work. I too
was hungry, but more for a restart, back to ten

days before, when walking sounded less broken.

*

## DATE NIGHT

Frustration and inconvenience crash "last call for alcohol,"
as if someone cried out, "is there a doctor in the house?"
As if they were both doctors. Frustration brings inconvenience
home. You hear their rattling bodies going at it in the kitchen.
You hear their angry love-making cry out like stuck mad dogs.
You hear them snore like grizzly things. Their conversation in
the morning, grunts and moans. They scratch where they can,
and hock up phlegm like mother birds regurgitate. The dishes
ring out, cereal and milk scatter and splash about table. They
crunch and moan and crunch and groan. And I watch them,
this couple born from circumstance. I feel they have fused in-
to me like an abomination. And I want to cut them off, clean.
They know this. Yet, they smile at me with a piranha's joy.

## WHERE THE BRAIN GOES
*(garbage head)*

*a)*

I think it all wrong.
I envision *Pet Sematary*.
Think Fred Gwynne sack-fallen
by the resurrected child who
sliced his Achilles. Then I see
Gwynne as Herman Munster,
throwing temper tantrums in
his black block shoes, jumping
up and down, shaking the house.
His Achilles supporting
his height, his weight.
I think Fred. I see two hims.
One tall. One floored.

*b)*

I believe it all wrong.
I go to the gambler maiming
the prize stallion. The sire
the owner will shoot to relieve
horse of misery—his cut tendon.
I think that. I think, "why
didn't they shoot me on
the basketball court?" My thinks
push out, like pus runs, or
some amoeba slithers in mud.

*c)*

I construe in the wrong.
In the grandest of murmurs
that sex can be accomplished
like I am twenty-two years
a buffer. Like a woman will ride
me out, bronco bust my
dark nads. It moves to mountain
oysters. From man to bull.
The cut. The cut to place
them on a plate, next to sauces
and dips. The cut. The cut.
Holding two testicles together,
then slicing them from body,
to roll out, individually.

*d)*

The stairs stretch longer. "Is this
a Freddie Kruger flick?" The closer
I get to them, the farther they slide
away. I see it all wrong. I see a priest
slapping concrete stairs in a Catholic
man's head, smashing into pain with
no inducement. I will do the same. Off-
balanced, or shaken by Linda Blair's
thirteen-year-old face, corrupted by
the hater of humans, as Hollywood
finds her a niche. I am thinking all wrong
on this. Maybe the meds are slurring
my brain. Maybe my blood pleads
too thin. Maybe the scriptures given
me have lost their meat, their bones.

## HOBBLER ODE

at break of day,
the first body I touch,

my two metallic arms
to navigate inconvenience.

at night's knock,
the last body I manage,

my two soul savers,
before dreaming me a little god.

## NOTES

The epigraph "the wheelchairs hate the shoes" comes from the poem "The Way of the World," by Kim Addonizio.

The title of the poem "Carol for Another Christmas" is taken from the 1964 movie of the same name.

## ACKNOWLEDGMENTS

This manuscript came to fruition because of Cheryl Scott-Fields, Liz Whiteacre, Katerina Stoykova-Klemer, Accents Publishing and the Accents Publishing staff, Frank X Walker, Leslie Anne Mcilroy, Michael Meyerhofer, and Derrick Harriell. I appreciate your service and want to thank you all for your help on bringing this baby into existence.

## ABOUT THE AUTHOR

Curtis L. Crisler's forthcoming poetry book, *"This" Ameri-can-ah*, will be released in 2015 (Cherry Castle Publishing). His books are *Pulling Scabs* (nominated for a Pushcart), *Tough Boy Sonatas* (YA), and *Dreamist: a mixed-genre novel* (YA), and his poetry chapbooks are *Wonderkind, Soundtrack to Latchkey Boy,* and *Spill*. He's been published in many magazines, journals, and anthologies. He is Associate Professor of English at Indiana University-Purdue University Fort Wayne, and a Cave Canem Fellow.

CPSIA information can be obtained
at www.ICGtesting.com
Printed in the USA
FFOW03n0503250215
11235FF